I READ! YOU READ!

Child's Turn to Read

Adult's Turn to Read

WE READ ABOUT

The Atlantic Ocean

By Lauren Gordon and Madison Parker

Table of Contents

SEAHORSE PUBLISHING

Parent and Caregiver Guide

Reading aloud with your child has many benefits. It expands vocabulary, sparks discussion, and promotes an emotional bond. Research shows that children who have books read aloud to them have improved language skills, leading to greater school success.

I Read! You Read! books offer a fun and easy way to read with your child. Follow these guidelines.

Before Reading

- Look at the front and back covers. Discuss personal experiences that relate to the topic.
- Read the *Words to Know* at the back of the book. Talk about what the words mean.
- If the book will be challenging or unfamiliar to your child, read it aloud by yourself the first time. Then, invite your child to participate in a second reading.

During Reading

CHILD Have your child read the words beside this symbol. This text has been carefully matched to the reading and grade levels shown on the cover.

ADULT You read the words beside this symbol.

- Stop often to discuss what you are reading and to make sure your child understands.
- If your child struggles with decoding a word, help them sound it out. If it is still a challenge, say the word for your child and have them repeat it after you.
- To find the meaning of a word, look for clues in the surrounding words and pictures.

After Reading

- Praise your child's efforts. Notice how they have grown as a reader.
- Use the *Comprehension Questions* at the back of the book.
- Discuss what your child learned and what they liked or didn't like about the book.

Most importantly, let your child know that reading is fun and worthwhile. Keep reading together as your child's skills and confidence grow.

The Atlantic Ocean

CHILD

There are five oceans on Earth.

One is the Atlantic Ocean.

Oceans are giant bodies of salt water.

ADULT

CHILD

The Atlantic Ocean is huge!

It touches North America and South America on one side.

It touches Europe and Africa on the other side.

ADULT

Over 70 percent of Earth's surface is covered by oceans. Of the five oceans, the most fish are caught in the Atlantic Ocean.

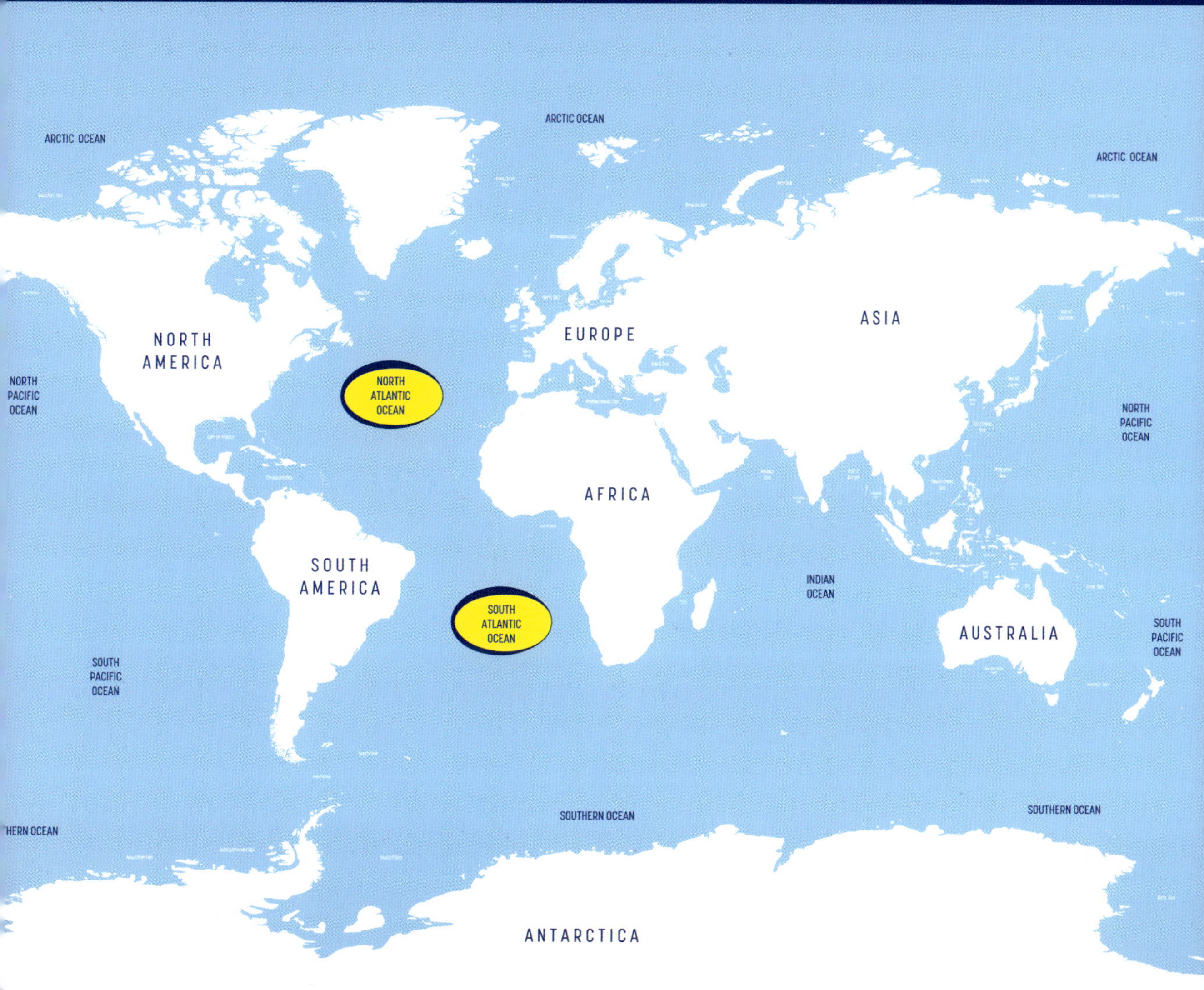
ARCTIC OCEAN
ARCTIC OCEAN
ARCTIC OCEAN
NORTH AMERICA
NORTH PACIFIC OCEAN
NORTH ATLANTIC OCEAN
EUROPE
ASIA
NORTH PACIFIC OCEAN
AFRICA
SOUTH AMERICA
SOUTH ATLANTIC OCEAN
INDIAN OCEAN
AUSTRALIA
SOUTH PACIFIC OCEAN
SOUTH PACIFIC OCEAN
SOUTHERN OCEAN
SOUTHERN OCEAN
HERN OCEAN
ANTARCTICA

There are many **islands** in the Atlantic Ocean.

Some are cold and icy.

Some have palm trees.

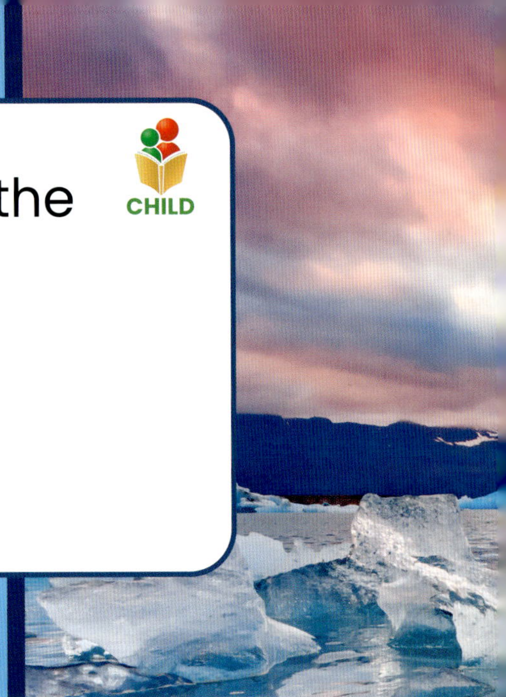

The Bahamas and Iceland are countries found on islands in the Atlantic Ocean.

ADULT

Tropical **islands**, such as Grand Bahama, are found in the South Atlantic Ocean. Islands with a colder **climate**, such as Iceland, are found in the North Atlantic Ocean.

This is Atlas Titan.
He is the reason
we call it the
Atlantic Ocean.

The word *Atlantic* comes from **ancient** Greek.

CHILD

It means "sea of Atlas."

ADULT

According to Greek mythology, Atlas must stand in the sea to hold up the pillars that keep heaven and Earth apart.

CHILD

The Atlantic Ocean is the world's second biggest ocean.

It is about the same size as seven United States of Americas put together!

ADULT

In some places, the Atlantic Ocean is 3,000 miles (4,830 kilometers) wide. It takes a cargo ship more than 20 days to travel the length of the Atlantic Ocean.

United States
Atlantic Ocean

The Atlantic Ocean is very deep.

It can be up to 28,000 feet (8,500 meters) deep.

That is over five miles (eight kilometers) deep!

Oceans have three major layers. The sunlight zone, at the top, gets light and heat from the sun. The twilight zone, in the middle, is darker and colder. The midnight zone, at the bottom, is always dark and cold.

CHILD

There are many types of animals that live in the Atlantic Ocean.

Some ocean animals have backbones, and some do not.

Animals with backbones are called **vertebrates**.

ADULT

Some Atlantic Ocean **vertebrates** are sea lions, manta rays, and narwhals. Animals that do not have backbones are invertebrates. Some Atlantic Ocean invertebrates are oysters, squid, and clams.

Manatees have backbones. Sea urchins do not.

CHILD

The small North Atlantic octopus hunts at the bottom of the ocean.

It likes cold, deep water.

ADULT

The North Atlantic octopus is so small that it could fit in the palm of your hand. It eats crabs, fish, and sea stars.

The North Atlantic octopus cannot survive in warm **climates**.

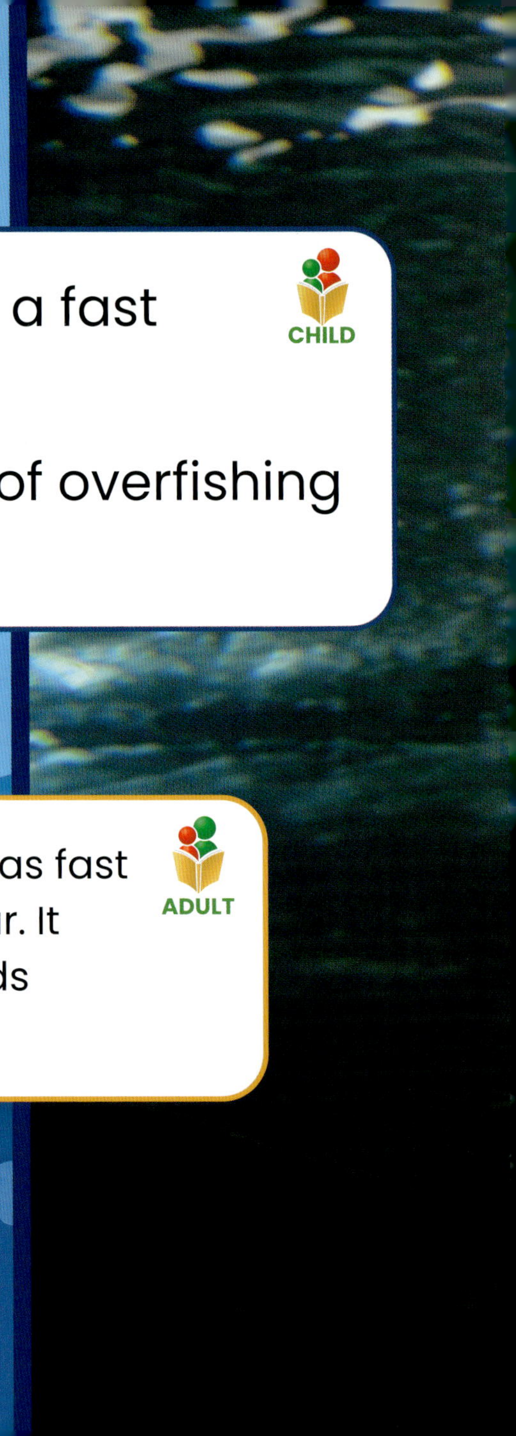

CHILD

The Atlantic bluefin tuna is a fast ocean swimmer.

It is **endangered** because of overfishing in the Atlantic Ocean.

ADULT

The Atlantic bluefin tuna can swim as fast as 43 miles (69 kilometers) per hour. It can weigh as much as 2,000 pounds (900 kilograms).

The population of Atlantic bluefin tuna is growing since laws have been made to protect it.

CHILD

The Atlantic Ocean is in danger.

Pollution from humans is hurting the ocean.

It is important to reduce, reuse, and recycle to help our oceans stay clean.

ADULT

People can help care for the Atlantic Ocean by participating in beach cleanups and using ocean-friendly sunscreen.

Words to Know

ancient (AYN-shuhnt): very old

climates (KLYE-mits): usual or typical weather patterns in an area over a long period of time

endangered (en-DAYN-jurd): at risk of extinction, often because of human activity

islands (EYE-luhnds): pieces of land completely surrounded by water

pollution (puh-LOO-shuhn): harmful materials that damage air, water, and soil, including gases, chemicals, and smoke

vertebrates (VUR-tuh-brates): animals with a backbone

Index

Comprehension Questions

1. True or False: The Atlantic Ocean is one of three oceans in the world.
2. True or False: There are many islands in the Atlantic Ocean.
3. True or False: The Atlantic Ocean gets its name from Atlas Titan.
4. True or False: The Atlantic Ocean is two feet deep.
5. True or False: The Atlantic Ocean is in danger due to pollution.

Answers
1. False 2. True 3. True 4. False 5. True

Written by: Lauren Gordon and Madison Parker
Design by: Jen Bowers
Editor: Kim Thompson

Library of Congress PCN Data
We Read About the Atlantic Ocean/ Lauren Gordon and Madison Parker
I Read! You Read!
ISBN 979-8-8873-5196-4 (hard cover)
ISBN 979-8-8873-5216-9 (paperback)
ISBN 979-8-8873-5236-7 (EPUB)
ISBN 979-8-8873-5256-5 (eBook)
Library of Congress Control Number: 2022945535

Printed in China

Photographs from Shutterstock.com: Cover and p.15 image ©2009 A Cotton Photo, backgound ©2012 Andrey_Kuzmin, water globe ©2012 zffoto; p.2 and throughout backgroud ©elic; p.3 and throughout background ©Aleksandra Bataeva, globes ©Designua; p.5 ©Pyty; p.6 ©2014 BlueOrange Studio; p.7 ©2019 Smit; p.8 ©2020 Rashbihari Dutta; p.11 ©2010 Chaykovsky Igor; p.13 ©2015 Rich Carey; p.15 ©2015 JGA; p.17 ©2015 Vladimir Wrangel; p.19 ©2019 jurgal photographer; p.21 ©2017 Richard Whitcombe

Seahorse Publishing Company
www.seahorsepub.com

Published in the United States
Seahorse Publishing
PO Box 771325
Coral Springs, FL 33077

SEAHORSE PUBLISHING